Unearned Privilege: Racial Ambiguity

By Mara Oso

Chapter One: Race as a Noun

If you think long enough about race, the less it makes sense. Differences of someone's face determines their character as much as chanting at an alter affects the moon's orbit.

What is race? Is it connected to one's culture; is it a determining factor of one's personality; or is it simply a grouping of Phenotypes attributed to an ethnic group as being the sole proprietor of that trait? Who knows? Well... I know. The third meaning is correct. However, even if it is simply phenotypes that could fit on any version of human, some people have attributed more to it. Some even went as far as to attribute race to intelligence, aggression and emotional connectivity. By doing this they have given power to shapes and colours.

Racial Categories do not exist unless someone believes that it does. Just like Religion, it has no power unless someone takes that belief and acts like it is real. Race had its uses in the past to justify atrocities. Race had its uses to justify education separation. Race had its uses to justify national division, movie roles, politicians, ambassadors and the list goes on and on. I am not going to continue to talk about how woefully idiotic it is that racial categories exist. The fact is, that it does, on every inch of this planet that is connected to the internet. Race, today, has very real consequences for very real people. Simply acting as if it doesn't exist is not a solution, its blissful ignorance. To truly get rid of race, we must address it, tear it apart, get rid of everything that came about because of it, and let it become yet another thing Humans in the past did.

Chapter Two: Race is not Culture.

Throughout Human History we have had interactions with groups of other humans. With the advent of Race, we gave these groups different names such as African, Asian, European, and Native American. Within these groups we have ethnicities such as Sub Saharan African, East and South East Asian, Oceania, Anglo-Saxon, and the list goes on. Then within even these we have cultures such as Mali Culture, Chinese Culture, Thai Culture, British,

French, and so on. Which over time became nation states surrounding these peoples linked with similar cultures and histories.

This is where the problem begins. There is an imaginary link between Race and Culture. Due to this imaginary link many connect their culture as being part of their race. In the United States of America (US) this issue is exceptionally present because those who were born "Pure Raced" in the US, with the caveat of being adopted or not being raised with such culture from their parents, feels the need to "reconnect" with "their" culture as if their "race" made it so.

Given the scenario of a Pure European Raced person, being born in China to a family whom have been in China since the Qing Dynasty. This Child of course would have Chinese culture because that is where he was born, that is where his parents were born and so on. It would be needlessly unfounded to say that this child needed to "be" European because of his race. His race and his culture has no connection, and by making the connection of race and culture, you not only forced this child to identify with people he has never even been around, but you are also making this child go through a crisis in his own identity. Due to his race not matching his culture.

Bringing me to the main topic of this book, Mixed People.

Chapter Three: Mixed People

Mixed People, Multiracial, Multiethnic, and the varying other creative names Pure Raced people have come up for them. Mixed Race people are what creates the idea of race into nonsense. If race were categories rather than simply a gradient of phenotypes (Even with this I have issues with), then mixed race people would not exist. Because categories are one or the other. A number can't be odd and even, a shape can't be both a rectangle and a triangle, and if race were actual categories like these are, then a person can't be both European and African.

Given this Scenario if race was an actual category then if we somehow could have a rectangle and a triangle reproduce, their offspring would have to be either a rectangle or a triangle. That is because these are actual categories, there are no over lapping. However, this is not the case in Humans. When two "Racial Categories" mix together you end up with a mixed child, someone somewhere in the middle of the spectrum. Due to this "Racial Categories" are much less categories than they are of descriptors, and very poor ones at that.

A mixed individual calling themselves all their "pieces" ignores the fact that these pieces are not able to interact and still be their original pieces. Going back to the prior example of Rectangles and Triangles, an Object cannot be both of these items, it is either one or the other or neither not both. This is of course a touchier subject when it comes to Humans, especially those of mixed race who feel that recognizing themselves as being pieces of a race is a part of who they are. However, going back to race being just a crude descriptor of phenotypes, hence trying to keep those descriptors does nothing more than add confusion to a person who should've been described as neither, rather than pieces in the first place.

Some multiracial individuals try to ignore this obvious error in judgement by saying that Race categories are in itself a gradient rather than sets of categories. Sure, we can say that. Though that brings up a complete new set of issues. Such as what is the gradient based on? Is it multiple gradients based on skin colour, hair curliness, hair colour, eye colour, nose length and width, when would this gradient no longer require more gradient wheels. Even if they were all figured out, when on this gradient you pass the threshold of being able to be called Asian, when two people next to each other on this gradient are called by two different races aren't we stating that the similarity between those two, who are right next to each other on the gradient, as being more dissimilar to one another than they are to someone on the other end of the category threshold.

Given this scenario to help illustrate the gradient error. We have a colour wheel of the colours on the visible spectrum. We observe one section the area between Yellow and Blue. In the area between we have the gradients of green. Within this green we select two colours that have a one degree of separation from one another. Now because of their location on this gradient one would be called Blue and the other would be called yellow, despite the two selected colours are closer to one another than they are to either Yellow or Blue. When applying this to Humans we have an issue where mixed people would be the colours of green rather than either of their two proponents. Making them not anything new put instead more related to someone within that range rather than to the thresholds that are being applied.

The main point of all of this is to drive home the fact that mixed people calling themselves by their parts, or by calling themselves completely one or the other ignored the fact that race doesn't work like that. Race doesn't really work at all to be honest, but given its current rules mixed people cannot without making a mess of this faulty word, justify being called by both of their races. Mixed people are just that, mixed. Allowing yourself to choose one or the other, or both, or neither is a privilege that only mixed people have. And it's a privilege because it is unearned, they didn't do anything to allow such racial fluid decisions, and allowing this fluidity brings up situation of pure raced people being able to do the same, especially if we are arguing that race doesn't exist, or wanting to get rid of it. Therefore, if humans are capable of doing it, then all humans should be given the opportunity to do the same.

Chapter Four: Mixed People and Culture

On a lighter note, because of how the current state of the world is right now, mixed people can assimilate more easily into multiple cultures than that of pure raced individuals. This of course if they learn the languages associated with said cultures. Because of this Mixed people are able to provide insight within multiple groups and avoid being an outsider among insiders as would those who were not in the same "racial category" would be. Mixed people in this aspect can seemingly be fluid with cultures and gather knowledge through personal experience rather than through second hand interactions.

Of course, with every good thing I must say the problem with this. The problem comes from that to perform these cultural practices in their authentic manner the mixed individual would have to ignore an entire family line of themselves as to avoid manipulating the culture to fit their racial needs. Mixed people, just by their very existence, creates compromises within cultures, slowly changing them until they are almost unrecognizable. Transformation and progression are good things; however, it is not good when the goal is to pass down traditions.

To avoid this alteration of cultures mixed people seemingly must adopt a new culture of being a middle person between the two races. Or, as I am a supporting of, getting rid of it in its entirety and focus on Science and World History Interactions and to let Pure Raced people be responsible of passing down those values and traditions. This is of course if people want to continue to associate culture with race. If you do, then this is what mixed people need to do to keep things non-counterintuitive. If you don't associate culture with race, then mixed people just like everyone else has the equal opportunity to have the culture that they desire.

Chapter Five: Mixed People to each other

It should not matter if someone is mixed with African and White, Asian and Native American, Black and Asian and so on, mixed people in this current world where race is a determining factor of interaction experience very similar situations.

Mixed Peoples have the unearned privilege of being asked what they are, unlike the pure raced peoples whom would never get this opportunity because strangers look at them and automatically put them into a category with no say.

Mixed People feel they need to make a choice to be the race of their father, or the race of their mother, as a sort of selecting your culture kind of test. Or could opt out of the selection process. Due to this being part of life, race becomes much less of a concrete thing and more of something that is just a feeling.

Mixed People have the privilege to speak for entire races of people that they themselves have a very loose connection to. The privilege to receive the benefits of being a certain race, as well as the benefit of opting out of the struggle of being that race, this is of course if you are a Grade A Garbage Person. But this ability still is an option open for mixed people to do.

Mixed People however, have no escape countries if the world does decide to perform a massive genocide on the minorities of their countries. Every mixed person is a minority in their country, even if they have the blood of a majority. Though if some South American Nations such as Brazil would accept Mixed Races of all kind, and allow that to stay how the majority of the population is, then that is a potential haven. But back to the point, in the case of "race wars" mixed people would be without a side to join.

Mixed People to another mixed person relieves the need to answer questions about their ancestry of heritage because there would be an understanding that they just feel mixed, not the races that they are mixed with. Of course, as I brought up before, culture can be very different among mixed people so that can always be a conversation starter.

The list can go on and on about the privileges that mixed people have that other races would not, all due to the fact of living "in between". However, plenty of videos have been made on the "feeling". The only thing I can add to it is that Mixed People are not victims, in many cases they are the object of obsession.

Chapter Six: Human Trophies

Pure Races suffer what I like to call *Feature Extremism*, which is when traits among a group of people just become more and more prominent over generations. Examples of this is like the flat faces found in some Asian people, or the Tiny Lips of Europeans or the Dark Skin in Africans. These features have their beauty among peoples in the group and those who have a fetish based on it. However, to the groups outside these traits are seen in not so good of a light.

Therefore, when mixed children are seen they serve as a sort of reminder that Human could be customized. That features that you do not like about yourself are able to be gotten rid of in your child. This frame of thinking not only reduces these humans to mere trophies, but for those who do love their traits, this makes mixed people seem nearly demon like. The existence of mixed people to them serve as a reminder that their "race" and identity are fragile and able to be gotten rid if not "protected".

Of course, both ways of thinking are unhealthy views of love... or attraction. Attraction should be based on the humans that you are currently, not on the humans you hope to produce. This may be a product from the demonization of altering your appearance. When people change an aspect of themselves it seems as a way of self-hatred. People who "love" their "race" see that any method of changing that, i.e. having a child with different features, as being a method of self-hatred. Those who don't like aspects of their race also seeks methods to changing it, and jump at the chance to claim a "Beautiful mixed" child as being part of them. As if this "mixed child" is proof that "beauty" can come from their DNA.

Compliments are not bad to receive, but blanket compliments on an entire "version" of human are bad, even if they are positive. No one is saying that you cannot have a preference, that's up to one's own prerogative, what I am saying is that this method of blanket complimenting carries more than just your preference. It creates a standard of beauty if you have enough influence. Because Beauty and Power are closely linked by stating that you like such and such feature now gives that feature more power over other, for no apparent reason than that it looks good.

Mixed people have an unearned privilege of attaining these standards of beauty, and being given the compliment of "so beautiful" simply by being born. This reduces their achievements to be the result of their attractiveness rather than their skill. If a "race" must work harder to achieve the same result, that's not the equality of opportunity. Mixed People, especially those in the US, have inflated the successes of the race that they claim to be. Due to this, a higher percentage of such race being in certain fields is not a true signal of development, but instead being the evidence that being attractive does give a person an extra privilege.

Chapter Seven: Religion makes things worse

In many cultures on Earth religion has been used to explain why there are certain races, and why certain races experience what they experience. This is of course because religion fills in the gaps where knowledge haven't gotten to explaining. In the ancient world race of course was one such of these things. How could early civilization explain why some humans looked different than the way they did. Of course, a being that created you, must have created them too. However, as with many religion, you simply can't make yourself the "bad guy" therefore that other group of people are and God is letting you know by marking them with an easily seen feature.

By appealing to a higher power to justify why some group of people are not doing so well, is a method of removing blame from one's own culture for either ignoring these people or using these people. On the other end, appealing to a higher power allows these races to live through their suffering in hopes that when they die they receive rewards proportional to their suffering.

Religion allows race to continue because it of course was created by a deity, and that deity does not make mistakes. Religion makes getting rid of Race in its entirety impossible simply because Humans should not have the power to undo what a deity has done.

Mixed people with this line of thinking alters religions to try and fit to everyone. These mixed people in history may have argued that their deity loves every kind of person because why would they want to be convinced that their god would doom them based on the "mark" on their skin, or feature of their hair, or the curve of their eyes.

This is most prevalent in religions that have "chosen people". Mixed people in those more ancient times would have altered the original intent to including all people rather than just the people that were being talked about in the original script. These early religions set what people are divinely born and which were not.

Religion set the stone in which race could be based on, people who look like this are my people, people who look like something else are something else. Despite in modern times we know that people are just that, people.

The mixing of people has made varying religion lose standards that were originally set. Such as what happen to people who never knew your deity, what happens if someone from the other group does more good then someone who is in your group, what happens to do whom are born part of your group but were raised by the other? All these may have been altered to what they are today by mixed people of the past to in a way allow themselves and whichever parent that was not part of the original to be allowed into their final resting place.

Main point here is that religion facilitates separation. A person would need to try and interpret religious text differently than others to allow people in general to have the chance at "paradise". With this religion this facilitation would not need to be done, and humans would just live as just that, humans.

Dehumanization, prejudice, and oppressions seemingly finds a way to be traced back to a religion. Which makes sense because humans cannot dehumanize one another without appealing to a higher power. Without this higher power, Humans lack the authority to justify why.

Religion, is okay for people to use as poetry, or novels, but not as a science book. Mixed people, if they were to create a culture of their own, I feel would try and shy away from religion in general or else over eons they would separate once again.

Chapter Eight: Human Traits

Individuals are not using race to decide if they like something or someone. Individuals typically, and honesty just want to see someone who looks like them achieve great things. Lately on Earth we have seen people who actively want to see someone who looks different from themselves not do so well, or in some cases fail.

This works very well to get "Pure raced" people into valuable positions and a lot of the support that they would need to achieve. In the US, the Asian communities there support heavily those of similar race. Though again, there is an issue that comes from this. When someone supposedly who is of their race, but don't have their traits. Such in the case within the same community of Eastern Asians not supporting South Eastern Asians, then it gets some degrees worse when an individual is mixed. Often phrases such as "not really" and "eh" gets used as if that is an indication of full support.

Humans are social animals and pay attention to what their environment says. Thus, to keep full support of their ambitions many people choose not to go outside of their "race" in order to continue to receive support. This disturbing practice, despite the world being connected since the Silk Road days, may be what continued our divide between one another. This need to support "One race". Again, it is innocent, it's a morale booster to see people that look like you achieve. In some crude way it could stimulate the taught that if you were in their position that you would achieve to.

Sadly, there is another negative. When you see someone, who looks like you get killed, that often makes you feel that if you were also in their position that you would have been killed too. Especially if it's a situation that is out of your control. This feeling also carries through people who looked like the person who caused the tragedy. The "race" that the person was that was killed now feel as victims and everyone who looks like the person who did the killing now has a relation to that killer.

Connecting with people based on their appearance being like yours is not wrong by any means. It just becomes wrong when those outside of your characteristics take on a personality based on what you observed.

Many people justify themselves by saying "better to be safe than sorry", "their communities are usually like this, so I am acting within their culture", or even the worse that I've heard "Look at the people in such and such place, if they were actually (blank) then wouldn't they as a whole be more successful." To this I must say, stop thinking like that. It doesn't make sense. Just because a genius was your race doesn't make you any smarter. Just because some murderer was your race doesn't make you a killer, just because some traveler was your race doesn't make you an explorer. There are much more important factors that determine how someone would end up, and the most important is socio-economics, much more than race.

To caveat on this, if a group of people have a lower socio-economic position than another overall, that nation and its actions is what made that situation occur, and the nation should address those. Nations are consumed with continued development, yet are willing to leave behind members of their citizenship. I don't know what it is with people, but when they assume someone is a certain kind of way, they are very willing to let that individual suffer. This willingness to allow a people to suffer simply people they are outside of the groups that you are in is likely why nations eventually collapse.

Mixed people, if nothing else, since they always were an outsider in their family and "racial group" then you must understand that individuals are distinctly different to mobs. That individuals are not defined by their characteristics, but instead by their actions in the situations they were in. That simply looking like someone does not make you related. But then again, the world we live in does still have race, so maybe the people you do look like define who you are. In which case unify with other mixed people to ultimately end the reason you needed to unite.

Liberals, Conservative, moderates, extremist, and the like, these are hardly descriptors of how people would act. When groups are formed people feel forced to join them. Certainly, there are people within these groups who agree with some opinions in the other. However, just like race, the feeling of being unsupported removes the feeling of being individualistic. The development of parties may actually be similar to how the development of race came about.

Chapter Nine: Where do we go from here?

Race, something that doesn't exist, however because of belief it sure does act powerful. Outside of the Western World, though we do not necessarily see race in the same context, what is seen is beauty. Due to features being an indication of beauty, this also put certain "races" with those features into the lowest version of beauty. It becomes racism when we begin to associate those feature with status and personalities. If there were an absents of this… I really don't know. It is such a world that is woefully different than ours that speculating on it would be to try and form a utopia by getting rid of a feature on our Earth that created to be this way.

Race doesn't exist. People see what they want to see. Intelligence comes from the size of your forehead as much as a more orange cup makes water taste like oranges. The way to get rid of "race" is not to act like it doesn't affect people's lives, it's to make it irrelevant. Mixed people have this Privilege to make this happen. By no longer calling themselves by their separate "races" as if there was an actual separation, but instead calling themselves by the name of the Unity, which right now is the crude word of mixed. Though I think a more appropriate one would be AContinen, meaning a person not from one continent.

I feel that mixed people are in the position to not be held down by the automatic perception of personality that pure raced people have. I feel that mixed people ought to try and advance Humanity in a direction that ignores those National Borders, and Racial Barriers. A unified mixed people could serve as the UN, that the UN never could be. An organization or state which focus is on Human Rights, rather than geopolitics. After stripping everything away that makes us different, what we do see is that we are all Humans.

www.ingramcontent.com/pod-product-compliance
Lightning Source LLC
Chambersburg PA
CBHW051401250726
48656CB00006B/2219